Well
with My
Soul

© 2013 by Barbour Publishing, Inc.

Written and compiled by Darlene Franklin.

Print ISBN 978-1-62416-140-7

eBook Editions:
Adobe Digital Edition (.epub) 978-1-62416-409-5
Kindle and MobiPocket Edition (.prc) 978-1-62416-408-8

Scripture quotations marked KJV are taken from the King James Version of the Bible.

Scripture quotations marked NIV are taken from the HOLY BIBLE, NEW INTERNATIONAL VERSION®. NIV®. Copyright © 1973, 1978, 1984, 2011 by Biblica, Inc.™ Used by permission. All rights reserved worldwide.

Scripture quotations marked CEB are taken from the Common English Bible®, CEB ® Copyright © 2010, 2011 by Common English Bible.™ Used by permission. All rights reserved worldwide.

Scripture quotations marked ERV are taken from the HOLY BIBLE: EASY-TO-READ VERSION © 2001 by World Bible Translation Center, Inc. and used by permission.

Scripture quotations marked ESV are from The Holy Bible, English Standard Version®, copyright © 2001 by Crossway Bibles, a publishing ministry of Good News Publishers. Used by permission. All rights reserved.

Published by Barbour Publishing, Inc., P.O. Box 719, Uhrichsville, Ohio 44683, www.barbourbooks.com

Our mission is to publish and distribute inspirational products offering exceptional value and biblical encouragement to the masses.

Member of the
Evangelical Christian
Publishers Association

Printed in the United States of America.

It Is
Well
with My
Soul

Inspiration from the Beloved Hymn

BARBOUR
PUBLISHING

Contents

It Is Well with My Soul

When peace, like a river, attendeth my way,
When sorrows like sea billows roll;
Whatever my lot, Thou has taught me to say,
It is well, it is well, with my soul.

Though Satan should buffet,
though trials should come,
Let this blest assurance control,
That Christ has regarded my helpless estate,
And hath shed His own blood for my soul.

My sin—oh, the bliss of this glorious thought—
My sin—not in part but the whole,
Is nailed to the cross, and I bear it no more,
Praise the Lord, praise the Lord, O my soul!

For me, be it Christ, be it Christ hence to live:
If Jordan above me shall roll,
No pang shall be mine, for in death as in life
Thou wilt whisper Thy peace to my soul.

But, Lord, 'tis for Thee, for Thy coming we wait,
The sky, not the grave, is our goal;
Oh trump of the angel! Oh voice of the Lord!
Blessed hope, blessed rest of my soul!

And Lord, haste the day when my faith shall be sight,
The clouds be rolled back as a scroll;
The trump shall resound, and the Lord shall descend,
Even so—it is well with my soul.

It is well, with my soul,
It is well, with my soul,
It is well, it is well, with my soul.

HORATIO G. SPAFFORD, 1873

Peace Like a River

"I will extend peace to her like a river,
and the wealth of nations like a flooding stream."
ISAIAH 66:12 NIV

The Romans defined peace—*pax*—as "*absentia belli,*" the absence of war. Today we might use *peace* as meaning an absence of disturbance or noise.

So what inspired Isaiah and, centuries later, the hymn writer Horatio G. Spafford, to compare peace to a river? Jesus described the new life He offered as "rivers of living water" that flowed from the inside out (John 7:38). The water of life flows like a river through heaven (Revelation 22:1).

Even small creeks and rivers must move. If they don't, they become stagnant and unable to support life. Grandfathers might take their grandchildren fishing to a quiet spot by a gently flowing stream. A few miles downstream that same river explodes into rapids as it pushes its way past rocks and beyond that, plunges into a waterfall.

A river represents movement—not an absence of disturbance. The truth is that turbulence brings life, even abundant life. Salmon fight their way upstream to spawn. Water surges over dams to provide electricity.

Instead of wishing for peace like that unmoving, stagnant pond, pray for the flowing river of God's living water that will bring life and peace.

*"Peace I leave with you. My peace I give you.
I give to you not as the world gives.
Don't be troubled or afraid."*
JOHN 14:27 CEB

*To us a child is born, to us a son is given,
and the government will be on his shoulders.
And he will be called Wonderful Counselor, Mighty God,
Everlasting Father, Prince of Peace.*
ISAIAH 9:6 NIV

*He was pierced for our transgressions,
he was crushed for our iniquities;
the punishment that brought us peace was
on him, and by his wounds we are healed.*
ISAIAH 53:5 NIV

Peace is not an absence of war,
but a virtue based on strength of character.
BARUCH SPINOZA

He who would live in peace and at ease must
not speak all he knows or all he sees.
BENJAMIN FRANKLIN

We look forward to the day when the Power of Love
will replace the Love of Power. Then will our
world know the blessings of peace.
WILLIAM E. GLADSTONE

In peace there's nothing so becomes
a man as modest stillness and humility.
WILLIAM SHAKESPEARE

And the fruit of righteousness is sown
in peace of them that make peace.
JAMES 3:18 KJV

My son, forget not my law; but let thine heart
keep my commandments: For length of days,
and long life, and peace, shall they add to thee.
PROVERBS 3:1–2 KJV

But the meek shall inherit the land and
delight themselves in abundant peace.
PSALM 37:11 ESV

And he shall be like a tree planted by the
rivers of water, that bringeth forth his fruit
in his season; his leaf also shall not wither;
and whatsoever he doeth shall prosper.
PSALM 1:3 KJV

The Gift of Peace

✳

Everlasting Father, thank You for Your Son, the
Prince of Peace. I thank You for the promise of
that peace to me. Forgive me when I allow the
anxiety in my heart to overpower Your peace.
Make the peace that is like a river flow in and
through me, that I may experience Your peace and
share it with others. May I grow in that peace by
obedience to Your will and Your
desires for my life. Amen.

Then the peace of God that exceeds
all understanding will keep your hearts
and minds safe in Christ Jesus.
PHILIPPIANS 4:7 CEB

There is a river whose streams make
glad the city of God, the holy place
where the Most High dwells.
PSALM 46:4 NIV

"If anyone believes in me, rivers of living
water will flow out from their heart.
That is what the Scriptures say."
JOHN 7:38 ERV

Lord, make me an instrument of Thy peace.
SAINT FRANCIS OF ASSISI

No God, no peace. Know God, know peace.
UNKNOWN

I could not live in peace if I put the shadow
of a willful sin between myself and God.
GEORGE ELIOT

After love comes peace. A great many people
are trying to make peace. But that has already
been done. God has not left it for us to do;
all that we have to do is to enter into it.
D. L. MOODY

When you have troubles, I am with you.
When you cross rivers, you will not be hurt.
ISAIAH 43:2 ERV

Those with sound thoughts you will keep in peace,
in peace because they trust in you.
ISAIAH 26:3 CEB

May the God of hope fill you with all joy
and peace in faith so that you overflow with
hope by the power of the Holy Spirit.
ROMANS 15:13 CEB

If thou shalt do this thing, and God
command thee so. . .all this people shall
also go to their place in peace.
EXODUS 18:23 KJV

Peace of God

✳

God, You offer me a peace that passes all
understanding. I admit that when trouble comes,
I often fail by not keeping You at the center of
my mind in simple faith and trust. Forgive me for
the times I allow sin to come between us.
Only by knowing Your peace for myself
can I offer it to others. Make me an
instrument of that peace. Amen.

I've got peace like a river; I've got love like an ocean;
I've got joy like a fountain in my soul.
AFRICAN AMERICAN SPIRITUAL

Like a river glorious is God's perfect peace.
Over all victorious, in its bright increase.
Perfect, yet it floweth fuller every day.
Perfect, yet it groweth deeper all the way.
FRANCES R. HAVERGAL

Peace, perfect peace, in this dark world of sin?
The blood of Jesus whispers peace within.
Peace, perfect peace, by thronging duties pressed?
To do the will of Jesus, this is rest.
E. H. BICKERSTETH

Sorrows Like
Sea Billows

*I cried by reason of mine affliction unto the L*ORD,
*and he heard me. . . . For thou hadst cast me into the deep,
in the midst of the seas. . .all thy billows and thy waves
passed over me.*
JONAH 2:2–3 KJV

Hymn writer Horatio Spafford may have wished he could change places with Jonah when he wrote the words to "It Is Well with My Soul." The prophet saved the lives of the sailors with him by sacrificing himself, and then God rescued him from the belly of the great fish after he repented.

Instead, Spafford faced a test of Job-like proportions. In 1871, the successful Christian businessman lost his son. The Chicago Fire wiped out his holdings on Lake Michigan. Two years later, last-minute business kept him at home while his wife and four daughters traveled ahead to Europe.

On the way across the Atlantic, another liner struck the Spafford women's ship. Spafford received a two-word cable from his wife: SAVED ALONE. On his own journey across the Atlantic to join her, he wrote the words "when sorrows like sea billows roll," and the hymn "It Is Well with My Soul" was born.

The longer we live, the more aware we become of the sorrows life's storms send rolling our way. Often, like Spafford, our sorrows involve losing family—parents, spouses, children—through disagreements, illness, even death.

Like Jonah, know that the Lord hears when we cry. If He casts us into the deep, He will also draw us out.

Deep calls to deep in the roar of your waterfalls;
all your waves and breakers have swept over me.
PSALM 42:7 NIV

A furious squall came up, and the waves broke
over the boat, so that it was nearly swamped. Jesus
was in the stern, sleeping on a cushion. The disciples
woke him and said to him, "Teacher, don't you care
if we drown?" He got up, rebuked the wind and said
to the waves, "Quiet! Be still!" Then the wind
died down and it was completely calm.
MARK 4:37–39 NIV

O what a blessed day that will be when I shall. . .
look back on the raging seas I have safely passed;
when I shall review my pains and sorrows, my fears and
tears, and possess the glory which was the end of all!
RICHARD BAXTER

Sorrow brings us closer to God than joys.
HENRY WARD BEECHER

Sorrow comes in great waves. . .but rolls over us,
and though it may almost smother us, it leaves us.
And we know that if it is strong, we are stronger,
inasmuch as it passes and we remain.
HENRY JAMES

Blessed are those who mourn,
for they will be comforted.
MATTHEW 5:4 NIV

[The Lord has anointed me to] provide for those
who grieve in Zion—to bestow on them a crown
of beauty instead of ashes, the oil of joy instead of
mourning, and a garment of praise instead of a spirit
of despair. They will be called oaks of righteousness,
a planting of the LORD for the display of his splendor.
ISAIAH 61:3 NIV

You calm the roaring seas; calm the
roaring waves, calm the noise of the nations.
PSALM 65:7 CEB

Waves of the Sea

✳

Sovereign Lord, Your hand controls everything—
from nature to my daily life. Yet when the waves
of life break over me, I stress, I doubt, I despair.
Forgive me. Out of the depths I call, and You
answer. You calm the waves that overwhelm me;
You comfort me. You make me strong and give
me joy. You cover me with Your peace in my
times of despair. Amen.

"*I assure you that you will cry and lament,
and the world will be happy. You will be sorrowful,
but your sorrow will turn into joy.*"
JOHN 16:20 CEB

*You answer us with awesome and righteous deeds,
God our Savior, the hope of all the ends of
the earth and of the farthest seas.*
PSALM 65:5 NIV

*The seas have lifted up, LORD, the seas have lifted up
their voice; the seas have lifted up their pounding waves.*
PSALM 93:3 NIV

Floods of joy o'er my soul like the sea billows roll,
since Jesus came into my heart.

Rufus McDaniel

Dear refuge of my weary soul,
On thee, when sorrows rise,
On thee, when waves of trouble roll,
My fainting hope relies.

Anne Steele

There is no despair so absolute as that which comes with
the first moments of our first great sorrow, when we have
not yet known what it is to have suffered and be healed,
to have despaired and to have recovered hope.

George Eliot

Earth has no sorrow that heaven cannot heal.

Thomas Moore

You have said, "I can't take it anymore! The LORD
has added sorrow to my pain. I'm worn out
from groaning and can find no rest."
JEREMIAH 45:3 CEB

You know I am very upset. You know how much I have
cried. Surely you have kept an account of all my tears.
PSALM 56:8 ERV

Those who sow with tears will reap with songs of joy.
Those who go out weeping, carrying seed to sow,
will return with songs of joy, carrying sheaves with them.
PSALM 126:5–6 NIV

The Certainty of Sorrow

✳

O God my Savior, since You are in control, why
do You allow waves of sorrow to crash over me?
I know that You promise not to send me any
burden too great to bear. Help me remember that
promise during times of sorrow. Keep my eyes
fixed on the joy that is to come. With the gift of
sorrow, teach me character and strength. Amen.

I trust in God. I know He cares for me,
On mountain bleak or on the stormy sea;
Tho' billows roll, He keeps my soul,
My heavn'ly Father watches over me.

W. C. MARTIN

Talents are best nurtured in solitude, but character
is best formed in the stormy billows of the world.

JOHANN WOLFGANG VON GOETHE

Sorrow is a fruit. God does not make it
grow on limbs too weak to bear it.

VICTOR HUGO

Whatever My Lot

I know that there is someone to defend me and that he lives!
And in the end, he will stand here on earth and defend me.
  After I leave my body and my skin has been destroyed,
  I know I will still see God. I will see him with my own eyes.
  I myself, not someone else, will see God. And I cannot
      tell you how excited that makes me feel!

JOB 19:25–27 ERV

The earliest written of biblical accounts, the book
of Job addresses the age-old question: Why do bad
things happen to good people?

Job had family, fortune, health. After Satan
received permission from God, all was stripped away.
Instead of complaining, Job said, "Blessed be the
name of the Lord." In the end, God restored Job's
earlier status.

When Job was in the middle, stuck between loss and restoration, his friends exhorted him to confess his sins. In defense of his innocence, he made a remarkable declaration of faith. "My redeemer lives! And He is my judge."

In good times and bad, when Job had friends aplenty as well as when everyone turned against him, he kept his eyes on the living God. The prospect of bringing his case before God excited him.

You may not experience a complete reversal of fortune like Job, but some days will seem better than others. Whatever your lot, make your daily prayer, "Blessed be the name of the Lord. I will see God—nothing can be more exciting!"

Job arose, tore his clothes, shaved his head, fell to the ground, and worshipped. He said: "Naked I came from my mother's womb; naked I will return there. The LORD has given; the LORD has taken; bless the LORD's name."
JOB 1:20–21 CEB

"Now what do you have here with you?
Give me five loaves of bread or whatever you can find."
1 SAMUEL 21:3 CEB

Then the LORD changed Job's fortune when
he prayed for his friends, and the LORD
doubled all Job's earlier possessions.
JOB 42:10 CEB

Though lowly here our lot may be,
High work have we to do,
In faith and trust to follow Him
Whose lot was lowly, too.

WILLIAM GASKELL

I am still determined to be cheerful and happy,
in whatever situation I may be; for I have also learned
from experience that the greater part of our
happiness or misery depends upon our dispositions,
and not upon our circumstances.

MARTHA WASHINGTON

Fate is not the ruler, but the servant of Providence.

EDWARD G. BULWER-LYTTON

*Turn to the L*ORD *for help in everything you do,*
and you will be successful.
PROVERBS 16:3 ERV

We know that God works all things together for
good for the ones who love God, for those
who are called according to his purpose.
ROMANS 8:28 CEB

In all the work you are given, do the best
you can. Work as though you are working
for the Lord, not any earthly master.
COLOSSIANS 3:23 ERV

Give thanks in all circumstances; for this
is God's will for you in Christ Jesus.
1 THESSALONIANS 5:18 NIV

Accepting God's Will

✳

Almighty God, I rest in Your sovereign care.
Everything that happens to me, good or bad,
You work in Your purpose for my life. Forgive
me for complaining about what You have given
me for today. Teach me to trust You in all that I
do. Keep my eyes focused on the Giver and
not on the gifts given. Amen.

You, Lord, are my portion, my cup;
you control my destiny.
PSALM 16:5 CEB

My body and my heart fail, but God is
my heart's rock and my share forever.
PSALM 73:26 CEB

This is the one good thing I've seen: it's appropriate
for people to eat, drink, and find enjoyment in all their
hard work under the sun during the brief lifetime
that God gives them because that's their lot in life.
ECCLESIASTES 5:18 CEB

[When] you eat the food of the land,
present a portion as an offering to the Lord.
NUMBERS 15:19 NIV

The roaring of lions, the howling of wolves, the raging
of the stormy sea, and the destructive sword,
are portions of eternity too great for the eye of man.
WILLIAM BLAKE

You are my forever.
You are my portion forever.
SHANE BARNARD

Accept the things to which fate binds you,
and love the people with whom fate brings
you together, but do so with all your heart.
MARCUS AURELIUS

A God without dominion, providence, and final causes,
is nothing else but fate and nature.
ALEXANDER POPE

Thou art my portion, O LORD; I have
said that I would keep Thy words.
PSALM 119:57 KJV

"He who is the Portion of Jacob is not like these, for he
is the Maker of all things, including Israel, the people
of his inheritance—the LORD Almighty is his name."
JEREMIAH 10:16 NIV

The LORD is my portion, saith my soul;
therefore will I hope in him.
LAMENTATIONS 3:24 KJV

Elijah said unto Elisha, Ask what I
shall do for thee. And Elisha said. . .
let a double portion of thy spirit be upon me.
2 KINGS 2:9 KJV

God Is My Portion

✳

Creator God, You are my portion. In You,
I have everything I need today, tomorrow,
and every day after. Forgive me for the times
I have called Your blessings in my life by
other names—like good luck. Forgive me for
complaining about my life. My hope is in You.
You are my fortress, my rock. Strengthen me
and keep Your words in my heart. Amen.

Thou my everlasting portion,
More than friend or life to me,
All along my pilgrim journey,
Savior, let me walk with Thee.

FANNY J. CROSBY

Socrates thought that if all our misfortunes were
laid in one common heap, whence every one must
take an equal portion, most persons would be
contented to take their own and depart.

PLUTARCH

What fates impose, that men must needs abide;
it boots not to resist both wind and tide.

WILLIAM SHAKESPEARE

Trials Should Come

*"I have told you these things so that you can have
peace in me. In this world you will have troubles.
But be brave! I have defeated the world."*

JOHN 16:33 ERV

A woman came to God with a complaint. "God, I feel
like You've given me the biggest cross. Please let me
exchange it for a smaller one."

With a gentle smile, God took the woman to a
closed door. "In this room, you will find everyone's
cross. You can choose the one you prefer to carry."

Walking into the room, the woman dropped her
burden on the ground. Some crosses reached to
the ceiling. She rushed past those. On other, smaller
ones, the wood was heavier. She didn't want those
either. As she examined the crosses, she rejected one
after another.

At last she found a small, insignificant cross, hidden under the weight of the others. Convinced she had made the best choice, she left the room.

When God saw her leave, He said, "That's the cross you carried in."

Trials will come. Jesus said so. The Bible talks about trials as if they are gifts from a loving Father. They produce joy, hope, and perseverance and prove genuine faith. But like the woman in the story, most people want to exchange their troubles for an easier load.

Every person has trials, or tests, fitted to her needs. Count your cross as a joy. Remember it is made for you.

*You now rejoice in this hope, even if it's necessary for
you to be distressed for a short time by various trials.
This is necessary so that your faith may be found
genuine. . . . Your genuine faith will result in praise, glory,
and honor for you when Jesus Christ is revealed.*
1 PETER 1:6–7 CEB

*They strengthened the disciples and urged
them to remain firm in the faith. They told them,
"If we are to enter God's kingdom, we must
pass through many troubles."*
ACTS 14:22 CEB

Trials teach us what we are; they dig up the soil,
and let us see what we are made of; they just turn
up some of the ill weeds onto the surface.

CHARLES SPURGEON

A gem cannot be polished without friction,
nor a man perfected without trials.

CHINESE PROVERB

May God give you. . .for every storm a rainbow,
for every tear a smile, for every care a promise,
and a blessing in each trial.

IRISH BLESSING

All trials are trials for one's life, just as
all sentences are sentences of death.

OSCAR WILDE

We even take pride in our problems, because we
know that trouble produces endurance, endurance
produces character, and character produces hope.
ROMANS 5:3–4 CEB

Search me, God, and know my heart;
test me and know my anxious thoughts.
PSALM 139:23 NIV

Each one should test their own actions.
Then they can take pride in themselves alone,
without comparing themselves to someone else.
GALATIANS 6:4 NIV

Endure hardship as discipline; God is treating
you as his children. For what children
are not disciplined by their father?
HEBREWS 12:7 NIV

The Gift of Tribulation

✳

Heavenly Father, You allowed Your own Son
to be tested—how can I expect anything less?
Even so, I confess that the thought of coming
trials and tribulations makes me tremble. I thank
You for the lessons each trial teaches me:
patience, perseverance, character, and hope.
Teach me to embrace them as Your testing
ground. Fill my heart to rejoice in Your gift.
Strengthen me with patience and hope.

*We didn't want any of you to be shaken
by these problems. You know very well
that we were meant to go through this.*
1 THESSALONIANS 3:3 CEB

*No temptation has seized you that isn't common
for people. But God is faithful. He won't allow you
to be tempted beyond your abilities. Instead,
with the temptation, God will also supply a way
out so that you will be able to endure it.*
1 CORINTHIANS 10:13 CEB

*Be happy because of the hope you have.
Be patient when you have troubles. Pray all the time.*
ROMANS 12:12 ERV

May you have enough happiness to keep
you sweet, enough trial to keep you strong,
enough sorrows to keep you human.
IRISH BLESSING

Fiery trials make golden Christians.
CHARLES SPURGEON

Virtue may be assailed, but never hurt, surprised by
unjust force, but not enthralled; yea even that which
mischief meant most harm—shall in the happy
trial prove most glory.
JOHN MILTON

As for courage and will—we cannot measure how much
of each lies within us, we can only trust there will be
sufficient to carry through trials which may lie ahead.
OVID

Consider it pure joy, my brothers and sisters, whenever you face trials of many kinds, because you know that the testing of your faith produces perseverance.

JAMES 1:2–3 NIV

Some time later God tested Abraham.

GENESIS 22:1 NIV

Then was Jesus led up of the Spirit into the wilderness to be tempted of the devil.

MATTHEW 4:1 KJV

The devil finished tempting Jesus in every way and went away to wait until a better time.

LUKE 4:13 ERV

Shaped by Trials

✳

Lord, I hate to admit it, but times of difficulty
shape me more than days of ease. Forgive me
for the times I seek to escape testing. I fear the
test, but Your promise that You will see us through
it lessens my worries. Nothing will come my
way that I can't handle with Your help.

Trials are medicines which our gracious and wise
Physician prescribes because we need them;
and He proportions the frequency and weight
of them to what the case requires. Let us trust
His skill and thank Him for His prescription.

Isaac Newton

What seems to us as bitter trials
are often blessings in disguise.

Oscar Wilde

Knowledge must come through action; you
can have no test, which is not fanciful, save trial.

Sophocles

Blessed Assurance

*Paul, a servant of God and an apostle of Jesus Christ
to further the faith of God's elect and their knowledge
of the truth that leads to godliness—in the hope of
eternal life, which God, who does not lie,
promised before the beginning of time.*

TITUS 1:1–2 NIV

Life insurance, health insurance, warranty, guarantee:
TV commercials and Internet ads shout these words
at us, but how reliable are these promises? Politicians
are particularly guilty of often promising something
they cannot deliver. In 1988, presidential candidate
George H. W. Bush famously promised, "Read my lips:
no new taxes." His opponents delighted when he
agreed to an increase in taxes two years later.

Fifty-one years before Bush, British Prime Minister Neville Chamberlain reached an agreement guaranteeing peace with Hitler. He told his countrymen, "I believe it is peace for our time. . . peace with honor." Within two years, Britain was pulled into the war.

The world craves certainty yet finds it an elusive quality. Promises given in good faith often cannot be kept. Four centuries ago French author Francois de la Rochefoucauld said, "The only thing constant in life is change."

Blessed assurance! One thing in life has not changed and never will: God is the same yesterday, today, and tomorrow. What He promises, He can and will perform. The Christian's hope is based on the unchanging God.

While we wait for the blessed hope—the appearing of the glory of our great God and Savior, Jesus Christ, who gave himself for us to redeem us from all wickedness and to purify for himself a people that are his very own, eager to do what is good.
TITUS 2:13–14 NIV

[The Holy Spirit] is a deposit guaranteeing our inheritance until the redemption of those who are God's possession—to the praise of his glory.
EPHESIANS 1:14 NIV

[God] put his Spirit in our hearts as a deposit, guaranteeing what is to come.
2 CORINTHIANS 1:22 NIV

The Christian's faith in Christ is trust in a living person, once crucified, dead, and buried, and now living forevermore. Call it, if you will, an assumption that ends as an assurance, or an experiment that ends as an experience, Christian faith is in fact a commitment that ends as a communion.

FREDERICK WARD KATES

Hope is some extraordinary spiritual grace that God gives us to control our fears, not to oust them.

VINCENT MCNABB

Hope is the word which God has written on the brow of every man.

VICTOR HUGO

Praise be to the God and Father of our Lord Jesus Christ.
God has great mercy, and because of his mercy he gave
us a new life. This new life brings us a living hope
through Jesus Christ's resurrection from death.

1 PETER 1:3 ERV

Therefore let all the house of Israel know assuredly,
that God hath made the same Jesus, whom ye
have crucified, both Lord and Christ.

ACTS 2:36 KJV

Surely he took up our pain and bore our suffering
yet we considered him punished by God,
stricken by him, and afflicted.

ISAIAH 53:4 NIV

Guaranteed for Eternity

✳

My God and Father, any hope I have in this life
comes from You. Your Son took my pain, my sin,
my weakness as His own. You have given me a
guarantee for eternal life, not on paper or because
of premiums I have paid, but through the blood of
Your Son and by Your Holy Spirit. Forgive me when I
doubt and my faith falters. Use me for Your glory.

*Surely goodness and mercy shall follow
me all the days of my life: and I will dwell
in the house of the LORD for ever.*
PSALM 23:6 KIV

*Surely his salvation is near those who fear him,
that his glory may dwell in our land.*
PSALM 85:9 NIV

*LORD, let your faithful love come to me—let your
salvation come to me according to your promise.*
PSALM 119:41 CEB

*And the work of righteousness shall be peace; and the
effect of righteousness quietness and assurance for ever.*
ISAIAH 32:17 KIV

Light for every darkness, life in death, the promise of our
Lord's return, and the assurance of everlasting glory.
D. L. Moody

The sense is, it is the Lord alone that saves and blesses:
and even though the whole mass of all evils should be
gathered together in one against a man, still, it is the
Lord who saves: salvation and blessing are in His hands.
Charles Spurgeon

If you say that God is good, great, blessed, wise,
or any such thing, the starting point is this: God is.
George Bernard Shaw

He said, "Surely they are my people, children who
will be true to me"; and so he became their Savior.
ISAIAH 63:8 NIV

"But those who trust in the LORD will be blessed.
They know that the LORD will do what he says."
JEREMIAH 17:7 ERV

Your promises have been thoroughly tested,
and your servant loves them.
PSALM 119:140 NIV

Your Word Is Enough

✳

Savior God, You are the eternal, great I Am, never
changing, always faithful. Your love, Your salvation—
Your Word is all the assurance I need. In You I find
light and life, peace and blessing. Forgive me for
the times I allow the noise of the world to drown
out Your sweet whispers. Teach me the truth that
You will do as You have promised.

Hope is the pillar that holds up the world.
Hope is the dream of a waking man.
PLINY THE ELDER

Blessed are the ears that hear the pulse of
the divine whisperer, and give no heed to
the many whisperings of the world.
THOMAS À KEMPIS

Yesterday, today, forever, Jesus is the same.
All may change, but Jesus never! Glory to His Name!
ALBERT B. SIMPSON

My Helpless Estate

Just as they came from their mother's womb naked, naked they'll
return, ending up just like they started. All their hard work
produces nothing—nothing they can take with them.
ECCLESIASTES 5:15 CEB

To get a glimpse of our helplessness as human beings, there are just two places you need to visit: a hospital's maternity unit and a nursing home.

A newborn baby relies on doctors, nurses, and then Mom and Dad to take care of her every need. Unable to feed, clothe, clean, or care for herself, there are dozens of basic necessities that she is helpless to do for herself—both physically and developmentally.

At the other end of life, she may need the assistance of nursing care when she needs help with the basics of personal care. The causes range from a debilitating illness such as multiple sclerosis or Alzheimer's disease, to accidents, to the physical ravages of old age.

Helpless when we're born into the world, we humans often again become helpless as death approaches. Solomon understood this truth well. At birth, he was naked and poor. At death, the same would be true. In between, whatever wealth or power he acquired—or lost—came from God.

The truth is, that no matter what helpless state you might be facing, God is still in control. He watches over us and protects us, especially when we are most vulnerable. The Lord cares deeply about our helpless estate—old, young, and in-between—and through it all, He acts on our behalf.

While we were still weak, at the right moment,
Christ died for ungodly people.

ROMANS 5:6 CEB

The law was without power because it was made
weak by our sinful selves. But God did what the law
could not do: He sent his own Son to earth with
the same human life that everyone else uses for sin.
God sent him to be an offering to pay for sin.
So God used a human life to destroy sin.

ROMANS 8:3 ERV

He gives strength to the weary and
increases the power of the weak.

ISAIAH 40:29 NIV

Helpless

✳

Holy God, how dare I come before You? I am
born sinful, weak, helpless, and foolish. How I
thank You for offering Your own Son to destroy
sin and its power over me. On my own, I cannot
overcome sin. You offer compassion and mercy
for my helpless estate. Forgive my sin, O Lord.
Make me obedient to Your Holy Spirit as He
transforms me into Your holy image.

LORD, get up and do something. Punish those
who are wicked, God. Don't forget those
who are poor and helpless.
PSALM 10:12 ERV

Now when Jesus saw the crowds, he had compassion
for them because they were troubled and helpless,
like sheep without a shepherd.
MATTHEW 9:36 CEB

Have mercy upon me, O LORD; for I am weak:
O LORD, heal me; for my bones are vexed.
PSALM 6:2 KJV

Watch ye and pray, lest ye enter into temptation.
The spirit truly is ready, but the flesh is weak.
MARK 14:38 KJV

There is a sacredness in tears. They are not the mark
of weakness, but of power. They speak more eloquently
than ten thousand tongues. They are messengers of
overwhelming grief. . .and unspeakable love.

WASHINGTON IRVING

All other ways of mortification are vain, all helps
leave us helpless, it must be done by the Spirit.

JOHN OWEN

We are born weak, we need strength; helpless,
we need aid; foolish, we need reason.

JEAN-JACQUES ROUSSEAU

*But God chose the foolish things of the world
to shame the wise; God chose the weak things
of the world to shame the strong.*
1 Corinthians 1:27 NIV

*Therefore, I'm all right with weaknesses, insults, disasters,
harassments, and stressful situations for the sake of
Christ, because when I'm weak, then I'm strong.*
2 Corinthians 12:10 CEB

*We are very weak, but the Spirit helps us with our
weakness. We don't know how to pray as we should,
but the Spirit himself speaks to God for us.*
Romans 8:26 ERV

As a Child

✳

Father, I depend on You. You desire me to come
to You like a child. Forgive me for my pride, for
rejoicing in my accomplishments, my strength,
my intellect. That is when I am the weakest and
most foolish of all. Make me weak, that I may
know Your strength. Reveal my foolishness, that
I may accept Your wisdom. May my soul long for
You as a child reaches for her father.

I had fainted, unless I had believed to see the
goodness of the LORD in the land of the living.
PSALM 27:13 KJV

I feel weaker and weaker as I wait for you to save me.
But I put my trust in your word.
PSALM 119:81 ERV

When my soul fainted within me I remembered the LORD:
and my prayer came in unto thee, into thine holy temple.
JONAH 2:7 KJV

But God demonstrates his own love for us in this:
While we were still sinners, Christ died for us.
ROMANS 5:8 NIV

Prayer is not asking. It is a longing of the soul. It is daily admission of one's weakness. It is better in prayer to have a heart without words than words without a heart.

MAHATMA GANDHI

The wise know too well their weakness to assume infallibility; and he who knows most, knows best how little he knows.

THOMAS JEFFERSON

If we do not know ourselves to be full of pride, ambition, lust, weakness, misery, and injustice, we are indeed blind. And if, knowing this, we do not desire deliverance, what can we say of a man?

BLAISE PASCAL

Then Asa called to the Lord his God and said, "Lord, there is no one like you to help the powerless against the mighty. Help us, Lord our God, for we rely on you, and in your name we have come against this vast army. Lord, you are our God; do not let mere mortals prevail against you."

2 Chronicles 14:11 NIV

For we do not have a high priest who is unable to empathize with our weaknesses, but we have one who has been tempted in every way, just as we are—yet he did not sin.

Hebrews 4:15 NIV

The Great High Priest

✳

Great High Priest, how can You sympathize with
my weaknesses? You are holy God, without
sin. Yet You became man. You experienced the
temptations that defeat me, but they didn't defeat
You. I know I am powerless to stop myself from
using the intelligence, strength, and will—all
presents from You—to do evil. Stop me in my
tracks, that I may recognize my sin and weakness.

To see helpless infancy stretching out her hands,
and pouring out her cries in testimony of dependence,
without any powers to alarm jealousy, or any
guilt to alienate affection, must surely awaken
tenderness in every human mind.

Samuel Johnson

For where the instrument of intelligence
is added to brute power and evil will,
mankind is powerless in its own defense.

Dante Alighieri

Weariness. Nothing is so insufferable to man as to be
completely at rest, without passions, without business,
without diversion, without study. He then feels his
nothingness, his insufficiency, his dependence,
his weakness, his emptiness.

Blaise Pascal

Shed His Own Blood

And almost all things are by the law purged with blood;
and without shedding of blood is no remission.
HEBREWS 9:22 KJV

How do you feel about blood? Does the sight of it
(or maybe just the thought of it) make you queasy?

Our twenty-first-century society has a fascination
with blood. Pop culture has romanticized the vampire
legend through books, movies, and TV shows.

But humankind's interest in blood isn't really a
new phenomenon. It extends far back in time. Many
world religions throughout history demand a blood
sacrifice. The ancient Aztecs even believed a human
heart torn from a living body was the only thing that
kept the sun rising every day.

In the twentieth century, doctors began the widespread practice of giving blood transfusions to patients who had lost a great deal of blood in accidents, disease, and during surgery. Without this infusion of new blood, death was inevitable.

Blood is associated with both life and death. How fitting, then, that the blood Jesus willingly gave on the cross meant both His death and our life. The power of His blemish-free, sinless blood holds the key to His resurrection and our everlasting life with Him in heaven. Hallelujah!

Is not the cup of thanksgiving for which we give thanks a participation in the blood of Christ? And is not the bread that we break a participation in the body of Christ?

1 CORINTHIANS 10:16 NIV

Whoever eats my flesh and drinks my blood remains in me, and I in them.

JOHN 6:56 NIV

God planned long ago to choose you and to make you his holy people, which is the Spirit's work. God wanted you to obey him and to be made clean by the blood sacrifice of Jesus Christ.

1 PETER 1:2 ERV

Relationship

✳

God, how I thank You that I am adopted into Your
family by the blood of Your Son. You chose me
as Your child before the foundation of the world.
Forgive me for the times I am a disobedient
daughter, when I live to please myself and not
You. Day by day, minute by minute, teach me to
remain in You and to serve You in all I do.

How much more will the blood of Jesus wash our consciences clean from dead works in order to serve the living God? He offered himself to God through the eternal Spirit as a sacrifice without any flaw.

HEBREWS 9:14 CEB

God is the one who raised from death our Lord Jesus, the Great Shepherd of his sheep. He raised him because Jesus sacrificed his blood to begin the new agreement that never ends. I pray that God will work through Jesus Christ to do the things in us that please him. To him be glory forever. Amen.

HEBREWS 13:20–21 ERV

See from His head, His hands, His feet,
Sorrow and love flow mingled down!
ISAAC WATTS

And can it be that I should gain an
interest in the Savior's blood?
Died He for me, who caused His pain—
for me, who Him to death pursued?
CHARLES WESLEY

This is all my hope and peace,
Nothing but the blood of Jesus.
ROBERT LOWRY

And so Jesus also suffered outside the city gate
to make the people holy through his own blood.
HEBREWS 13:12 NIV

Through his faithfulness, God displayed Jesus as the
place of sacrifice where mercy is found by means of
his blood. He did this to demonstrate his righteousness
in passing over sins that happened before.
ROMANS 3:25 CEB

Brothers and sisters, we have confidence that we can
enter the holy of holies by means of Jesus' blood.
HEBREWS 10:19 CEB

Holy of Holies

✴

Holy Lord, why do You, who are so great and holy, desire communion with me? You love me so much that You chose pain, suffering, and death to bring me close to You. Forgive me when I spurn my redemption by choosing to sin.

"The blood will be your sign on the houses where you live. Whenever I see the blood, I'll pass over you. No plague will destroy you when I strike the land of Egypt."
EXODUS 12:13 CEB

"This is my blood of the covenant, which is poured out for many so that their sins may be forgiven."
MATTHEW 26:28 CEB

You have come to Jesus—the one who brought the new agreement from God to his people. You have come to the sprinkled blood that tells us about better things than the blood of Abel.
HEBREWS 12:24 ERV

There is power, power, wonder-working power,
in the precious blood of the Lamb.

LEWIS E. JONES

Incomprehensible and immutable is the love of God.
For it was not after we were reconciled to Him by the
blood of His Son that He began to love us, but He
loved us before the foundation of the world, that with
His only begotten Son we, too, might be sons of
God before we were anything at all.

AUGUSTINE OF HIPPO

*For you know that it was not with perishable things
such as silver or gold that you were redeemed from
the empty way of life handed down to you from your
ancestors, but with the precious blood of Christ,
a lamb without blemish or defect.*
1 Peter 1:18–19 NIV

*Behold the Lamb of God, which taketh
away the sin of the world.*
John 1:29 KJV

*But now in Christ Jesus you who once were far away
have been brought near by the blood of Christ.*
EPHESIANS 2:13 NIV

Power in the Blood

✦

Lamb of God, You love me. I cannot comprehend
such a love, that You would offer Yourself in my
place. I thank You for the hope and peace that are
mine through Your sacrifice. Forgive me when I
rely on my own strength to save myself. Keep me
under Your blood. When trials come, remind me to
trust in Your love, Your grace, and Your power.

Keep me, Savior, from day to day;
Under the precious blood.
ELIZA E. HEWITT

This is faith: a renouncing of everything we are
apt to call our own and relying wholly upon the
blood, righteousness, and intercession of Jesus.
JOHN NEWTON

Although believers by nature are far from God
and children of wrath, even as others, yet it is
amazing to think how nigh they are brought to
Him again by the blood of Jesus Christ.
GEORGE WHITEFIELD

My Sin Is
Nailed to the Cross

Who will bring any charge against those whom God has chosen? It is God who justifies. Who then is the one who condemns? No one. Christ Jesus who died—more than that, who was raised to life—is at the right hand of God and is also interceding for us.

ROMANS 8:33–34 NIV

A mother hears the sound of glass breaking. She runs into the living room to learn what has happened.

Her favorite lamp, a delicate porcelain base holding the light bulb and shade, is shattered, scattered across the floor. Two guilty figures surround the mess: her six-year-old and her two-year-old.

The boys look at each other, and in unison they point to each other. "He did it."

In that instant, the mother wishes she had a video camera to replay the last few minutes in the living room. But all she can do is question her children and decide who is lying and who is telling the truth.

Like Lady Justice, the mother seeks to administer justice blindly, without favoritism.

God doesn't need blinders. He sees the scales of justice clearly. The only weight equal to sin is death; and Jesus' death equals the weight of all sin for all time. In God's courtroom, He is judge, prosecutor, and defense counsel.

Your sin. His cross. He paid the price—for you.

Now if someone is guilty of a capital crime,
and they are executed, and you then hang them
on a tree, you must not leave the body hanging
on the tree but must bury it the same day because
God's curse is on those who are hanged.
DEUTERONOMY 21:22–23 CEB

Christ took away that curse. He changed places with
us and put himself under that curse. The Scriptures say,
"Anyone who is hung on a tree is under a curse."
GALATIANS 3:13 ERV

The blood of Jesus Christ his Son
cleanseth us from all sin.
1 JOHN 1:7 KJV

He Died For Me

Savior God, the men You used to write Your
Word exhausted language in describing Your
sacrifice: death, offering, cursed, crushed,
suffering, nailed, atoned, Lamb of God. You
gave Your very life to restore me to fellowship
with You and to satisfy the sin debt I owed.
Forgive me when I ask forgiveness without
regard to the cost. Use me in the ministry of
reconciliation, to bring my neighbor close to You.

*"Once a year Aaron must make a special sacrifice.
He will use the blood of the sin offering to erase
the sins of the people. . . . This day will be
called the Day of Atonement."*
EXODUS 30:10 ERV

*It was the LORD's will to crush him and cause him to
suffer, and though the LORD makes his life an offering
for sin, he will see his offspring and prolong his days.*
ISAIAH 53:10 NIV

*He humbled himself by becoming obedient to
the point of death, even death on a cross.*
PHILIPPIANS 2:8 CEB

To abandon all, to strip one's self of all, in order to seek
and follow Jesus Christ naked to Bethlehem where He
was born, naked to the hall where He was scourged,
and naked to Calvary where He died on the cross, is so
great a mystery that neither the thing nor the knowledge
of it, is given to any but through faith in the Son of God.

JOHN WESLEY

What a wonderful, wonderful Savior,
Who would die on the cross for me!
Freely shedding His precious lifeblood,
That the sinner might be made free.

FREDERICK A. GRAVES

*God forbid that I should glory, save in the cross
of our Lord Jesus Christ, by whom the world
is crucified unto me, and I unto the world.*
GALATIANS 6:14 KJV

*Christ is our peace. . . . With his body, he broke
down the barrier of hatred that divided us.*
EPHESIANS 2:14 CEB

*Through him to reconcile to himself all things. . .
by making peace through his blood, shed on the cross.*
COLOSSIANS 1:20 NIV

*He destroyed the record of the debt we owed. . . .
He canceled it by nailing it to the cross.*
COLOSSIANS 2:14 CEB

Nail-Scarred Hands

✳

Merciful God, on the cross You not only paid for
my sin, You also made me anew. You changed me,
so that I am no longer a slave to sin. Forgive me
when I live as though nothing has changed. Like
Thomas, I say I won't believe unless I see proof.
Forgive my doubt. Open my eyes and my heart
to Your will, that I may become like Christ.

*For we know that our old self was crucified with him
so that the body ruled by sin might be done away with,
that we should no longer be slaves to sin.*

ROMANS 6:6 NIV

*For he hath made him to be sin for us, who knew no sin;
that we might be made the righteousness of God in him.*

2 CORINTHIANS 5:21 KJV

*In that day there shall be a fountain opened to
the house of David and to the inhabitants of
Jerusalem for sin and for uncleanness.*

ZECHARIAH 13:1 KJV

Our method of proclaiming salvation is this:
to point out to every heart the loving Lamb,
who died for us, and although He was the
Son of God, offered Himself for our sins.

COUNT ZINZENDORF

They are nailed to the cross! They are nailed to the cross!
Oh, how much He was willing to bear!
With what anguish and loss Jesus went to the cross,
But He carried my sins with Him there.

CARRIE E. BECK

He paid a debt He did not owe;
I owed a debt I could not pay.

ELLIS J. CRUM

The Blood deals with what we have done,
whereas the Cross deals with what we are.
The Blood disposes of our sins, while the Cross
strikes at the root of our capacity for sin.

WATCHMAN NEE

Oh beloved, oh beloved; nailed unto the
cross for me, O what sin hast Thou
committed; Thou who callest all to be?

SAINT TAKLA CHURCH

I Bear It No More

> *"Come to me, all you who are weary and burdened, and I will give you rest. Take my yoke upon you and learn from me, for I am gentle and humble in heart, and you will find rest for your souls. For my yoke is easy and my burden is light."*
> MATTHEW 11:28–30 NIV

Does your exercise routine include lifting weights? Maybe you tone a little bit with a dumbbell or two, or maybe you spend a few minutes after cardio on a weight machine. Some female Olympic weightlifters have lifted more than four hundred pounds in their events. Talk about a heavy burden.

Not many women are weightlifters, but we all know what it means to carry a heavy load. It may mean a literal load such as a child on our back and grocery bags in each hand. It may be a burdened schedule, juggling family, work, and ministry. It may be emotional baggage from the past. Everyone carries the load of sin and earns its paycheck, death.

What are you burdened with today?

Most of us would welcome someone to share the yoke, to help carry the load. In Jesus, we find the perfect weightlifting partner—because He takes it all. He gives rest to the weary. He won't reprimand us for being too weak. He removes our heavy weight of sin and returns a light burden in its place.

Go to Him—or better yet, ask Him to come to you if you can't carry your burden any farther—and find rest for your soul.

*And Cain said unto the L*ORD,
My punishment is greater than I can bear.
GENESIS 4:13 KJV

They will bear their guilt—the prophet will
be as guilty as the one who consults him.
EZEKIEL 14:10 NIV

They show that the requirements of the law are
written on their hearts, their consciences also bearing
witness, and their thoughts sometimes accusing them
and at other times even defending them.
ROMANS 2:15 NIV

"So you must bear your shame. You have made
your sisters look good compared to you."
EZEKIEL 16:52 ERV

For consequences of past sin,
Effect doth every follow cause;
If we sow tares, we reap not grain,
For such are nature's laws.

ARDELIA COTTON BARTON

One carries the sins of his forebears as one
carries their features in his face. One bears
their blood, and their honor or their blight.

GUILLERMO DEL TORO & CHUCK HOGAN

Must Jesus bear the cross alone,
and all the world go free?

THOMAS SHEPHERD

*"I myself will guarantee his safety. . . . If I do not bring
him back to you and set him here before you,
I will bear the blame before you all my life."*
GENESIS 43:9 NIV

*Just as we have borne the image of the earthly man,
so shall we bear the image of the heavenly man.*
1 CORINTHIANS 15:49 NIV

*"For they tie together heavy packs that are impossible
to carry. They put them on the shoulders of others,
but are unwilling to lift a finger to move them."*
MATTHEW 23:4 CEB

More Than I Can Bear

Father, You wrote Your law on my heart, even though it's something I can't memorize in church. Trying and failing to obey, the consequences of disobedience are more than I can bear. Forgive me when I continue trying to conquer the addiction of sin on my own. Teach me to rest in the arms of Jesus, to live in the forgiveness that has destroyed sin's power in my life.

"If you sin and break any of the commands that the LORD said must not be done, you are guilty. Even if you did not know about it, you are still responsible."
LEVITICUS 5:17 ERV

Only the one who sins will die. A child won't bear a parent's guilt, and a parent won't bear a child's guilt. Those who do right will be declared innocent, and the wicked will be declared guilty.
EZEKIEL 18:20 CEB

"I took the load from your shoulder. . . . When you were in trouble, you called for help, and I set you free."
PSALM 81:6–7 ERV

I must tell Jesus! I must tell Jesus!
I cannot bear my burdens alone;
I must tell Jesus! I must tell Jesus!
Jesus can help me, Jesus alone.

ELISHA A. HOFFMAN

Safe in the arms of Jesus, safe from corroding care, safe
from the world's temptations, sin cannot harm me there.

FANNY J. CROSBY

Sin in its ordinary progress first *deceives*,
next *hardens*, and then *destroys*.

JOHN THORNTON

All sins tend to be addictive, and the
terminal point of addiction is damnation.

W. H. AUDEN

*I will bear the indignation of the L*ORD*, because I have
sinned against him, until he plead my cause, and
execute judgment for me: he will bring me forth to
the light, and I shall behold his righteousness.*
MICAH 7:9 KJV

*So Christ was sacrificed once to take away the sins of
many; and he will appear a second time, not to bear sin,
but to bring salvation to those who are waiting for him.*
HEBREWS 9:28 NIV

*"The servant's master took pity on him,
canceled the debt and let him go."*
MATTHEW 18:27 NIV

Remembered No More

God Who seeks me, You marked my sin debt
PAID IN FULL at Calvary, and one day You will
return to complete the work of salvation. You
put my sins in a locked box and tossed them
to the bottom of the ocean, never again to be
remembered. Forgive me when I continue to sin,
to deny Your ownership of my life. Teach me
to forgive others as You have forgiven me.

*After his deep anguish he will see light,
and he will be satisfied. Through his knowledge,
the righteous one, my servant, will make
many righteous, and will bear their guilt.*
ISAIAH 53:11 CEB

*"Why do you try to test God by putting on the
necks of Gentiles a yoke that neither we nor
our ancestors have been able to bear?"*
ACTS 15:10 NIV

*Because for thy sake I have borne reproach;
shame hath covered my face.*
PSALM 69:7 KJV

Sin is its own punishment,
devouring you from the inside.
WILLIAM PAUL YOUNG

Sinners are made up of contradictions:
contradictions to truth and reason, to God,
to themselves, and to one another.
BENJAMIN WHICHCOTE

The first step in a person's salvation
is knowing of their sin.
SENECA

Sin is basically a denial of
God's right of possession.
EDWIN LOUIS COLE

Let sinners be wiped clean from the earth;
let the wicked be no more. But let my whole
being bless the LORD! Praise the LORD!
PSALM 104:35 CEB

"I, even I, am he who blots out your transgressions,
for my own sake, and remembers your sins no more."
ISAIAH 43:25 NIV

"No longer will they teach their neighbor, or say
to one another, 'Know the LORD,' because they will
all know me, from the least of them to the greatest,"
declares the LORD. "For I will forgive their wickedness
and will remember their sins no more."
JEREMIAH 31:34 NIV

Hence to Live

*So I beg you, brothers and sisters, because of the great
mercy God has shown us, offer your lives as a living
sacrifice to him—an offering that is only for God and
pleasing to him. Considering what he has done, it is
only right that you should worship him in this way.*

ROMANS 12:1 ERV

In the Old Testament, when a priest made a sacrifice
of a blemish-free animal, it meant that animal's
death. So for Paul to encourage the church in Rome
to offer their lives as a living sacrifice to God, the
term may have seemed like an oxymoron.

The truth is, because of what Jesus did on the
cross, He has every right to require a sacrifice from
us. But if we gave up everything—even our very
lives—it wouldn't fulfill the debt we owe Him.

Instead, we can live as living sacrifices by dedicating our lives—our years here on earth—to give glory to Him. That could mean something life-changing like going into full-time mission work, sharing the good news to the ends of the earth. But maybe today that means sharing with someone in need in the name of Jesus. Or it might mean taking an extra moment to chat with a coworker who is having a rough day and then praying for her.

Considering what Jesus has done, offering yourself as a living sacrifice is only right and natural. Today, live like Christ, for Christ, by faith in Christ, and you'll find an abundant life in Him.

For to me to live is Christ, and to die is gain.
PHILIPPIANS 1:21 KJV

*As a result, they do not live the rest of their earthly lives
for evil human desires, but rather for the will of God.*
1 PETER 4:2 NIV

*Be very careful, then, how you live—
not as unwise but as wise.*
EPHESIANS 5:15 NIV

*Then the LORD your God will circumcise your hearts
and the hearts of your descendants so that you love
the LORD your God with all your mind and with all
your being in order that you may live.*
DEUTERONOMY 30:6 CEB

My life, my love, I give to Thee,
Thou Lamb of God, who died for me.
Oh, may I ever faithful be,
My Savior and my God!

C. R. DUNBAR

Our mind is where our pleasure is, our heart is where our
treasure is, our love is where our life is, but all these, our
pleasure, treasure, and life, are reposed in Jesus Christ.

THOMAS ADAMS

The determining factor of my
existence is no longer my past.

SINCLAIR FERGUSON

*"So my heart is happy, and the words I speak are
words of joy. Yes, even my body will live with hope."*
ACTS 2:26–27 ERV

"The righteous will live by faith."
ROMANS 1:17 NIV

*"I am come that they might have life,
and that they might have it more abundantly."*
JOHN 10:10 KJV

*Live like free people, but don't use your freedom as an
excuse to do evil. Live as those who are serving God.*
1 PETER 2:16 ERV

Role Model

✳

"I Am," the eternal, living God, in You I have
abundant life, a life that looks to my future in
Christ and not my past pain and sin. Your love
compels me to give my life back to You. With
God's Son as my example and empowered by
the Holy Spirit, I have no excuse for not doing
Your will. Forgive me when I choose to live
the old way, and not in Your Spirit.

*If we be dead with Christ, we believe
that we shall also live with him.*
ROMANS 6:8 KJV

*If we say we live in God,
we must live the way Jesus lived.*
1 JOHN 2:6 ERV

*It is true that Christ was weak when he was killed
on the cross, but he lives now by God's power.
It is also true that we share his weakness, but in
dealing with you, we will be alive in him by God's power.*
2 CORINTHIANS 13:4 ERV

If we live by the Spirit, let's follow the Spirit.
GALATIANS 5:25 CEB

If, then, you are looking for the way you should go,
take Christ, because He Himself is the way.

THOMAS AQUINAS

When Christ is the center of your focus,
all else will come into proper perspective.

CROFT M. PENTZ

This is the great reward of service, to live, far out
and on, in the life of others; this is the mystery of
Christ—to give life's best for such high sake that
it shall be found again unto life eternal.

JOSHUA CHAMBERLAIN

So I am not the one living now—it is Christ living in me.
I still live in my body, but I live by faith in the Son of God.
GALATIANS 2:20 ERV

As a prisoner for the Lord, then, I urge you to live
a life worthy of the calling you have received.
EPHESIANS 4:1 NIV

"He follows my decrees and faithfully keeps my laws.
That man is righteous; he will surely live."
EZEKIEL 18:9 NIV

I died to the Law through the Law,
so that I could live for God.
GALATIANS 2:19 CEB

My All in All

✳

Lover of my soul, Your hands hold the universe
together. When I look at You, everything falls into
place. You promise that if I seek You, I will find
You. You are the Way when I seek my path. You
are my Light when I've lost my way. Without You,
I am nothing. With You, I have all that I need.
Take my life in Your service. Amen.

He died for the sake of all so that those who
are alive should live not for themselves but
for the one who died for them and was raised.
2 CORINTHIANS 5:15 CEB

Seek the LORD, and ye shall live.
AMOS 5:6 KJV

Christ carried our sins in his body on the cross.
He did this so that we would stop living
for sin and live for what is right.
1 PETER 2:24 ERV

In Death as in Life

O death, where is thy sting? O grave, where is thy victory? The sting of death is sin; and the strength of sin is the law. But thanks be to God, which giveth us the victory through our Lord Jesus Christ.

1 Corinthians 15:55–57 KJV

Death finds everyone. It claims the elderly, at the end of a full life. It claims the youngest ones who die before they are even born. It claims people at every age in between.

Like a young woman—just twenty-four years old—who passed away suddenly. People filled the sanctuary for her memorial service, shocked at the loss of the sweet-spirited girl. The house of worship was transformed into an assembly of mourners.

The pastor shared the girl's testimony in her own words. Her poetic expression of faith lifted grief into the realm of rejoicing. "I look into Your face / a face of love and wonder / I shall find a place called home in Your arms." No one listening could doubt that she had gone on to her heavenly home. This death was not a final good-bye, but only a temporary separation.

As Paul admonished the Thessalonians, the mourners rejoiced as those with hope. They celebrated the victory given to the Christian through the Lord Jesus Christ.

Sooner or later, unless we are still living when Jesus returns, all Christians will experience death. But because of His sacrifice on the cross, death has lost its sting. The grave no longer has the final word in the story of our lives. Thanks be to God!

Precious in the sight of the
LORD is the death of his saints.
PSALM 116:15 KIV

So choose life! Then you and your children will live.
You must love the LORD your God and obey him.
Never leave him, because he is your life.
DEUTERONOMY 30:19–20 ERV

He destroyed death and brought life and
immortality into clear focus through the good news.
2 TIMOTHY 1:10 CEB

Jesus died for us so that we can live together
with him. It is not important if we are
alive or dead when Jesus comes.
1 THESSALONIANS 5:10 ERV

I'll love Thee in life, I will love Thee in death,
And praise Thee as long as Thou givest me breath;
And say when the death dew lies cold on my brow,
If ever I loved Thee, My Jesus, 'tis now.

WILLIAM R. FEATHERSTONE

If Jesus Himself shall be our leader,
We shall walk through the valley in peace.

AFRICAN AMERICAN SPIRITUAL

See in what peace a Christian can die.

JOSEPH ADDISON

*Therefore, we were buried together with him through
baptism into his death, so that just as Christ was raised
from the dead through the glory of the Father,
we too can walk in newness of life.*
ROMANS 6:4 CEB

*We are confident, I say, and would prefer to be
away from the body and at home with the Lord.*
2 CORINTHIANS 5:8 NIV

*To every thing there is a season, and a time
to every purpose under the heaven:
A time to be born, and a time to die.*
ECCLESIASTES 3:1–2 KJV

Perfect Peace

✴

Peace-giving God, I have seen the peace that
presides at the death of loved ones who know
You. When I walk through that valley, whether
in the shadows of someone else's passing,
or as I take my final journey, You will give me
the same peace. Forgive me when I fear death,
as those who have no hope. Glorify Yourself
in me, both in life and in death.

*I eagerly expect and hope that I will in no way be
ashamed, but will have sufficient courage so that
now as always Christ will be exalted in my body,
whether by life or by death.*

PHILIPPIANS 1:20 NIV

*The teaching of the wise is a fountain of life,
turning a person from the snares of death.*

PROVERBS 13:14 NIV

*We don't live for ourselves and we don't die
for ourselves. If we live, we live for the Lord,
and if we die, we die for the Lord. Therefore,
whether we live or die, we belong to God.*

ROMANS 14:7–8 CEB

So send I you—to leave your life's ambitions,
To die to dear desire, self-will resign,
To labor long and love where men revile you,
So send I you—to lose your life in Mine.

E. MARGARET CLARKSON

Peace, perfect peace, death shadowing us and ours?
Jesus has vanquished death and all its powers.

E. H. BICKERSTETH

For death is no more than a turning
of us over from time to eternity.

WILLIAM PENN

St. Teresa of Avila described our life in this
world as like a night in a second-class hotel.

MALCOLM MUGGERIDGE

"It will bring light to those who live in darkness, in the fear of death. It will guide us into the way that brings peace."
LUKE 1:79 ERV

The fear of the LORD is a fountain of life,
to depart from the snares of death.
PROVERBS 14:27 KJV

We want you to know about people who have
died so that you won't mourn like others who don't
have any hope. Since we believe that Jesus died
and rose, so we also believe that God will bring
with him those who have died in Jesus.
1 THESSALONIANS 4:13–14 CEB

Time and Eternity

✳

Alpha and Omega, Lord of the living and the
dead, You have conquered my final, greatest
enemy. Thank You that death is now my portal
into Your eternal presence. I look forward to
the day when You will wipe all tears from my
eyes, as a mother comforts her child. I pray for
those who do not yet believe in You, that they
will receive the good news with joy.

*The attitude that comes from selfishness
leads to death, but the attitude that comes
from the Spirit leads to life and peace.*

ROMANS 8:6 CEB

*"I assure you, anyone who hears what I say and
believes in the one who sent me has eternal life.
They will not be judged guilty. They have already
left death and have entered into life."*

JOHN 5:24 ERV

*That is why Christ died and rose from death to live
again—so that he could be Lord over those
who have died and those who are living.*

ROMANS 14:9 ERV

The Sky Is Our Goal

If you would tear open the skies and come down to earth, then everything would change. . . . No one has ever seen any God except you, who does such great things for those who trust him.

ISAIAH 64:1, 4 ERV

It's humanity's universal cry: "God, if only You would act. . ."

Mary and Martha appealed to their good friend, the miracle-worker Jesus, to come when their brother lay dying. They *knew* what Jesus could do. But Jesus didn't come, and Martha could only say, "Lord, if you had been here, my brother would not have died" (John 11:21 ERV).

Like Isaiah, who also knew what God could do, Martha couldn't see any reason for Jesus' silence. Today's reader knows the rest of the story, that Jesus raised Lazarus from the dead, and the glory was given to God. But for Mary and Martha, the days they spent waiting seemed cruelly long.

That's where Christians live in this world—between the agony of Good Friday and the final answer of the Resurrection—between the new life received at salvation and the future new heaven and new earth, when all things will be made new.

So we wait for the return of her Savior. Living by faith, we anticipate the end of the story. But we know the final score. Death is only the portal to eternity—eternity with our heavenly Father.

Live today in the hope of the day when God will tear open the skies and every eye on earth shall see Him.

"Why are you standing here looking into the sky?
You saw Jesus carried away from you into heaven.
He will come back in the same way you saw him go."
ACTS 1:11 ERV

"Skies, listen and I will speak.
Earth, hear the words of my mouth."
DEUTERONOMY 32:1 ERV

"I will return and take you to be with
me so that where I am you will be too."
JOHN 14:3 CEB

If the earthly tent we live in is destroyed,
we have a building from God, an eternal
house in heaven, not built by human hands.
2 CORINTHIANS 5:1 NIV

The second coming of Christ is the completion
of His saving work. If you take it away,
the whole fabric of His saving work unravels.

JOHN PIPER

When, by the gift of His infinite grace,
I am accorded in heaven a place,
Just to be there and to look on His face,
Will thru the ages be glory for me.

CHARLES H. GABRIEL

Onward to the prize before us!
Soon His beauty we'll behold.
Soon the pearly gates will open,
We shall tread the streets of gold.

ELIZA E. HEWITT

"There before me was one like a son of man,
coming with the clouds of heaven. He approached
the Ancient of Days and was led into his presence."
DANIEL 7:13 NIV

He that sitteth in the heavens shall laugh:
the LORD shall have them in derision.
PSALM 2:4 KJV

The day when the Lord comes again will surprise
everyone like the coming of a thief. The sky will
disappear with a loud noise. Everything in the sky
will be destroyed with fire. And the earth and
everything in it will be burned up.
2 PETER 3:10 ERV

Going Home

✦

Beautiful Savior, one day I will come to the home
You have prepared for me. I long to see beloved
ones again, but nothing compares to the time I
will see You face-to-face. Nothing will ever come
between us again. Forgive me for living as though
this earth is my final destination. May You, the
author and finisher of my faith, be my goal,
a heavenly crown, the prize I seek.

Then shall they see the Son of man coming
in the clouds with great power and glory.
MARK 13:26 KJV

The LORD hath prepared his throne in
the heavens; and his kingdom ruleth over all.
PSALM 103:19 KJV

"All the peoples of the earth will mourn when
they see the Son of Man coming on the clouds
of heaven, with power and great glory."
MATTHEW 24:30 NIV

I press on toward the goal to win the prize for which
God has called me heavenward in Christ Jesus.
PHILIPPIANS 3:14 NIV

Precisely because we cannot predict the moment,
we must be ready at all moments.
C. S. LEWIS

The apostolic church thought more about the
Second Coming of Jesus Christ than about death
and heaven. The early Christians were looking,
not for a cleft in the ground called a grave but
for a cleavage in the sky called Glory.
ALEXANDER MACLAREN

Soon He's coming back to welcome me
Far beyond the starry sky.
LUTHER B. BRIDGERS

*We which are alive and remain shall be caught up
together with them in the clouds, to meet the Lord
in the air: and so shall we ever be with the Lord.*
1 THESSALONIANS 4:17 KJV

*Sell your possessions and give to those in need. Make for
yourselves wallets that don't wear out—a treasure in
heaven that never runs out. No thief comes near there.*
LUKE 12:33 CEB

*Therefore, since we have a great high priest
who has ascended into heaven, Jesus the Son
of God, let us hold firmly to the faith we profess.*
HEBREWS 4:14 NIV

That Will Be Glory

✳

Glorious King, the day is coming soon when You
will return with power and glory to begin Your
perfect rule. I can't miss it; everyone will see You.
Forgive me for the times I live as if I don't look
forward to Your return. Teach me to keep watch
at all times; open the eyes of those who
are not ready to meet their King.

"Look, he is coming with the clouds," and "every eye will see him, even those who pierced him"; and all peoples on earth "will mourn because of him." So shall it be! Amen.

REVELATION 1:7 NIV

"Pour down, you heavens above, and let the clouds flow with righteousness. Let the earth open for salvation to bear fruit; let righteousness sprout as well. I, the LORD, have created these things."

ISAIAH 45:8 CEB

The highest heaven belongs to the LORD, but he gave the earth to all people.

PSALM 115:16 CEB

The Voice of the Lord

*Behold, I stand at the door, and knock: if any man
hear my voice, and open the door, I will come in
to him, and will sup with him, and he with me.*

REVELATION 3:20 KJV

Picture the sight: a mother holds her newborn baby, crooning in a quiet voice, "I love Jordan." The baby girl learns her identity through that soft voice.

When that infant has grown into an active toddler, she scribbles on the walls. The first time, her mother corrects her gently. "Jordan, use crayons on paper, not on the walls."

Jordan continues coloring. Her mother's voice grows more urgent. "Jordan Elizabeth, I told you to stop coloring on the walls."

Ignoring the correction, Jordan continues. Speaking even more forcefully, the mother says, "JORDAN ELIZABETH FRANKLIN, go to time out NOW."

The Christian's relationship with God the Father works a lot like that. He longs to speak to us in the still, small voice that Elijah heard in the cave (1 Kings 19:12). He wants His children to open the door and invite Him in for a time of fellowship (Revelation 3:20).

However, if believers don't listen, God can always get louder. He will do whatever is necessary to get their attention. And in the last day, God will come with a shout. Every eye will see Him and every ear will hear. Those who have never paid attention to His voice before will fall on their knees, terrified.

Second Peter 3:9 (NIV) says, "The Lord is not slow in keeping his promise, as some understand slowness. Instead he is patient with you, not wanting anyone to perish, but everyone to come to repentance." Listen to God's still, small voice—before it becomes a shout.

To him that rideth upon the heavens of heavens. . .
he doth send out his voice, and that a mighty voice.
PSALM 68:33 KJV

While he was still speaking, look, a bright cloud
overshadowed them. A voice from the cloud said,
"This is my Son whom I dearly love."
MATTHEW 17:5 CEB

The LORD God goes up to his throne
at the sound of the trumpet and horn.
PSALM 47:5 ERV

He will send his angels with the sound of
a great trumpet, and they will gather his
chosen ones from the four corners of the earth.
MATTHEW 24:31 CEB

God's voice is still and quiet and easily
buried under an avalanche of clamor.
CHARLES STANLEY

God is gone up with a merry noise:
and the *Lord* with the sound of the trump.
BOOK OF COMMON PRAYER

Praise the Lord, praise the Lord,
Let the earth hear His voice!
FANNY CROSBY

At the sound of God's voice, the heavenly waters roar.
God raises the clouds from the ends of the earth.

JEREMIAH 51:16 CEB

"When he has brought out all his own, he goes on
ahead of them, and his sheep follow him because
they know his voice."

JOHN 10:4 NIV

In a moment, in the twinkling of an eye, at the last
trump: for the trumpet shall sound, and the dead
shall be raised incorruptible, and we shall be changed.

1 CORINTHIANS 15:52 KJV

The LORD thundered from the sky;
God Most High let his voice be heard.

PSALM 18:13 ERV

Still, Small Voice

✳

Lord, You came to me, not with a war cry, but in a
still, small voice. You still speak to the innermost
recesses of my heart, where words are no longer
needed. I thank You that You shower me with loving
words and song. Forgive me when I turn a deaf ear
to Your voice. Let me live so that one day I will hear
"Well done, My good and faithful servant."

The Lord thunders at the head of his army;
his forces are beyond number, and mighty
is the army that obeys his command.
JOEL 2:11 NIV

For the Lord himself shall descend from heaven with
a shout, with the voice of the archangel, and with
the trump of God: and the dead in Christ shall rise first.
1 THESSALONIANS 4:16 KJV

For he is our God; and we are the people of his
pasture, and the sheep of his hand. To day if
ye will hear his voice, Harden not your heart.
PSALM 95:7–8 KJV

Oh, there is something in that voice that
reaches the innermost recesses of my spirit!
HENRY WADSWORTH LONGFELLOW

Then He'll call me some day to His home far away,
Where His glory forever I'll share.
GEORGE BENNARD

O, blow your trumpet, Gabriel,
Blow your trumpet louder;
And I want that trumpet to blow me home
To my new Jerusalem.
AFRICAN AMERICAN SPIRITUAL

*The LORD God will shout from Zion. He will shout
from Jerusalem, and the sky and the earth will shake.
But the LORD God will be a safe place for his people.
He will be a place of safety for the people of Israel.*

JOEL 3:16 ERV

*The LORD's voice can be heard over the sea.
The voice of our glorious LORD God is like thunder
over the great ocean. The LORD's voice is powerful.
It shows the LORD's glory.*

PSALM 29:3–4 ERV

Majesty and Power

✳

Creator God, the same voice that called the world
into being still calls today. At the sound of Your
voice, the world trembles. I thank You that You will
put me in a safe place during the time of judgment.
Forgive me when I don't listen unless You shout.
Tune my ear to Your voice. Fill my heart with
longing for the day when You call me home.

*After the earthquake a fire; but the L*ORD *was not in the fire: and after the fire a still small voice.*
1 KINGS 19:12 KJV

*The L*ORD *will march out like a champion. . .*
with a shout he will raise the battle cry
and will triumph over his enemies.
ISAIAH 42:13 NIV

*The L*ORD *of heavenly forces will come to you*
with thunder, earthquake, and a mighty voice,
with whirlwind, tempest, and flames of devouring fire.
ISAIAH 29:6 CEB

*My Faith Shall
Be Sight*

*The city does not need the sun or the moon to shine on it,
for the glory of God gives it light, and the Lamb is its lamp.*

REVELATION 21:23 NIV

The Last Battle, the final volume in the classic
Chronicles of Narnia by C. S. Lewis, tells the end
of the old Narnia. Everyone is sent to their proper
place, except for a group of dwarves. They remain in
the stable, where they only see darkness. Lucy begs
Aslan to help them.

In sorrow, the great Lion replies, "They will not
let us help them. They have chosen cunning instead
of belief. . .so afraid of being taken in that they
cannot be taken out." They have chosen to shut their
eyes to the light of Aslan's country.

Put yourself in the dwarves' place. They are only inches away from glory—but they have blinded themselves to it—too afraid to be taken advantage of.

God's glory shines in the earth today. He can be seen in the face of a newborn baby, in the splendor of a sunset—in the fellowship of believers gathered in His name.

Open your eyes to God's glory on this earth. Resist the temptation of becoming cynical and jaded toward His many miracles. Being aware of His presence, His holiness, His glory, will prepare your heart for an eternity in His full greatness.

All these great people continued living with faith until they died. They did not get the things God promised his people. But they were happy just to see those promises coming far in the future.
HEBREWS 11:13 ERV

For we walk by faith, not by sight.
2 CORINTHIANS 5:7 KJV

Faith is the reality of what we hope for, the proof of what we don't see.
HEBREWS 11:1 CEB

[Jesus] said, "I am the light of the world. Whoever follows me will never live in darkness. They will have the light that gives life."
JOHN 8:12 ERV

What a pleasure in life it is bringing!
What assurance and hope ever bright!
Oh, what rapture and bliss are awaiting,
When our faith shall be lost in the sight!
BARNEY E. WARREN

Death is no more than passing from one room into
another. But there's a difference for me, you know.
Because in that other room I shall be able to see.
HELEN KELLER

Faith is to believe what you do not yet see;
the reward for this faith is to see what you believe.
SAINT AUGUSTINE

Now we see a reflection in a mirror; then we will see face-to-face. Now I know partially, but then I will know completely in the same way that I have been completely known.

1 CORINTHIANS 13:12 CEB

We must never stop looking to Jesus. He is the leader of our faith, and he is the one who makes our faith complete. . . . He accepted the shame of the cross as if it were nothing because of the joy he could see waiting for him.

HEBREWS 12:2 ERV

Now and Then

✳

Eternal, invisible God, I long for the day
when my faith shall be sight. I am blessed to
be among the number who didn't see Your Son
on earth and yet have believed. I thank You,
because even the faith that allows me to "see"
is a gift of Your grace. Forgive my doubts; I live
between Your promise and the fulfillment.
Show me the joy that lies ahead of this life.

And without faith it is impossible to please God, because
anyone who comes to him must believe that he exists
and that he rewards those who earnestly seek him.
HEBREWS 11:6 NIV

Then Jesus told him, "Because you have seen me,
you have believed; blessed are those who
have not seen and yet have believed."
JOHN 20:29 NIV

Jesus answered, "Philip, I have been with
you for a long time. So you should know me.
Anyone who has seen me has seen the Father too.
So why do you say, 'Show us the Father'?"
JOHN 14:9 ERV

That, when our life of faith is done,
In realms of clearer light
We may behold Thee as Thou art,
With full and endless sight.
HENRY ALFORD

Faith will vanish into sight;
Hope be emptied in delight;
Love in heaven will shine more bright;
Therefore, give us Love.
CHRISTOPHER WADSWORTH

In faith there is enough light for those who want to
believe and enough shadows to blind those who don't.
BLAISE PASCAL

I do not believe this darkness will endure.
J. R. R. TOLKIEN

Taste and see that the Lord is good;
blessed is the one who takes refuge in him.
PSALM 34:8 NIV

The man answered, "I don't know if he is a sinner.
But I do know this: I was blind, and now I can see."
JOHN 9:25 ERV

"And blessed is she that believed:
for there shall be a performance of those
things which were told her from the Lord."
LUKE 1:45 KJV

Who really believed what we heard?
Who saw in it the Lord's great power?
ISAIAH 53:1 ERV

I See in Part

✴

All-seeing God, You have given me eyes to see.
I already see hints of Your goodness, I hear
rumors of Your power. Improve my spiritual vision,
tune my hearing to the frequency of Your voice.
Forgive the times that I choose to be blind and
deaf. May I live today in Your faith, hope, and love,
awaiting the day when You make all things new.

"He will wipe away every tear from their eyes. Death will
be no more. There will be no mourning, crying, or pain
anymore, for the former things have passed away."
Then the one seated on the throne said, "Look! I'm
making all things new." He also said, "Write this down,
for these words are trustworthy and true."

REVELATION 21:4–5 CEB

The blind receive their sight, and the lame walk, the lepers
are cleansed, and the deaf hear, the dead are raised up,
and the poor have the gospel preached to them.

MATTHEW 11:5 KJV

*It Is Well
with My Soul*

Praise the LORD, my soul; all my inmost being,
praise his holy name. Praise the LORD, my soul,
and forget not all his benefits.

PSALM 103:1–2 NIV

In Psalm 103, David gave at least one reason per verse why the believer should praise God with all her soul.

Perhaps hymn writer H. G. Spafford thought of David's words when he wrote the hymn, "It Is Well with My Soul."

Consider the words of the song with Psalm 103 in mind:

- It is well with my soul because God "satisfies [my] desires with good things" (verse 5).
- My soul is in good standing with God because "[He] redeems [my] life from the pit and crowns [me] with love and compassion" (verse 4).

- I know what is right and good, because God's righteousness is made available to those "who keep His covenant and remember to obey His precepts" (verse 18).
- I am living well, because God "forgives all [my] sins and heals all [my] diseases" (verse 3).

In spite of everything Spafford endured in the loss of his children and his fortune, when he considered everything God had done in the past and would do in the future, he repeated, "It is well with my soul."

When you are feeling far from "well," take a look at Spafford's hymn and David's psalm. You will come away with the assurance that with the help of the Holy Spirit, it can be well with your soul.

*I will praise thee; for I am fearfully and
wonderfully made: marvellous are thy works;
and that my soul knoweth right well.*
PSALM 139:14 KJV

*Be merciful unto me, O God, be merciful unto me: for my
soul trusteth in thee: yea, in the shadow of thy wings will
I make my refuge, until these calamities be overpast.*
PSALM 57:1 KJV

*Return unto thy rest, O my soul; for the LORD
hath dealt bountifully with thee. For thou hast
delivered my soul from death, mine eyes
from tears, and my feet from falling.*
PSALM 116:7–8 KJV

At Rest

✷

In You, Father, my soul finds rest, only in You.
Because my hope is anchored in You, it reaches
behind the curtain that used to separate us.
Forgive me when I allow worries, physical distress,
or circumstances to cloud that assurance.
Encourage me with the miracle of my creation,
Your attention to each detail of my being. Make
me still before You; let Your praise fill my mouth.

Dear friend, I pray that you may enjoy
good health and that all may go well with you,
even as your soul is getting along well.
3 JOHN 2 NIV

God, I am ready, heart and soul,
to sing songs of praise.
PSALM 57:7 ERV

I am waiting for the LORD to help me.
My soul waits for him. I trust what he says.
PSALM 130:5 ERV

We have this hope as an anchor for the soul, firm and
secure. It enters the inner sanctuary behind the curtain.
HEBREWS 6:19 NIV

What is soul? It's like electricity—we don't really
know what it is, but it's a force that can light a room.

RAY CHARLES

Be still, my soul: when change and tears are past,
All safe and blessed we shall meet at last.

KATHARINA A. VON SCHLEGEL

There is gladness in my soul today,
And hope, and praise, and love,
For blessings which He gives me now,
For joys laid up above.

ELIZA E. HEWITT

Why waste your money on something that is not real food?
Why should you work for something that does not really
satisfy you? Listen closely to me and you will eat what is
good. You will enjoy the food that satisfies your soul.
ISAIAH 55:2 ERV

I delight greatly in the LORD; my soul rejoices in my
God. For he has clothed me with garments of salvation
and arrayed me in a robe of his righteousness, as a
bridegroom adorns his head like a priest, and as
a bride adorns herself with her jewels.
ISAIAH 61:10 NIV

Salt and Light

✳

Divine Bridegroom, my soul looks forward to our
wedding supper. In You, I find everything good,
both now and forevermore. Forgive me when
I dine only on things that satisfy the body; fill
me with food that satisfies my soul. May I take
nourishment from Your Word. While I am waiting,
make me as a vessel to shed Your light and
sprinkle salt across the world.

My heart, O God, is steadfast;
I will sing and make music with all my soul.
PSALM 108:1 NIV